READERS

STAR WARS

BATTLE FOR
NABOO

Lisa Stock

DK READERS

Level 3

Level 4

A Note to Parents

DK READERS is a compelling program for beginning readers, designed in conjunction with leading literacy experts, including Dr. Linda Gambrell, Distinguished Professor of Education at Clemson University. Dr. Gambrell has served as President of the National Reading Conference, the College Reading Association, and the International Reading Association.

Beautiful illustrations and superb full-color photographs combine with engaging, easy-to-read stories to offer a fresh approach to each subject in the series. Each DK READER is guaranteed to capture a child's interest while developing his or her reading skills, general knowledge, and love of reading.

The five levels of DK READERS are aimed at different reading abilities, enabling you to choose the books that are exactly right for your child:

Pre-level 1: Learning to read
Level 1: Beginning to read
Level 2: Beginning to read alone
Level 3: Reading alone
Level 4: Proficient readers

The "normal" age at which a child begins to read can be anywhere from three to eight years old. Adult participation through the lower levels is very helpful for providing encouragement, discussing storylines, and sounding out unfamiliar words.

No matter which level you select, you can be sure that you are helping your child learn to read, then read to learn!

DK

LONDON, NEW YORK, MUNICH,
MELBOURNE, AND DELHI

Editor Lisa Stock
Designer Sandra Perry
Design Manager Ron Stobbart
Publishing Manager Catherine Saunders
Art Director Lisa Lanzarini
Publisher Simon Beecroft
Publishing Director Alex Allan
Production Editor Marc Staples
Production Controller Kara Wallace
Jacket Designer Jon Hall
Reading Consultant Dr. Linda Gambrell

For Lucasfilm
Executive Editor J. W. Rinzler
Art Director Troy Alders
Keeper of the Holocron Leland Chee
Director of Publishing Carol Roeder

First American Edition, 2012

Published in the United States by DK Publishing
375 Hudson Street, New York, New York 10014

12 13 14 15 16 10 9 8 7 6 5 4 3 2 1
001—183090—02/12

DK books are available at special discounts when purchased in bulk
for sales promotions, premiums, fund-raising, or educational use.
For details, contact:
DK Publishing Special Markets
375 Hudson Street
New York, New York 10014
SpecialSales@dk.com

A catalog record for this book is available
from the Library of Congress.

ISBN: 978-0-7566-9007-6 (Hardback)
ISBN: 978-0-7566-9008-3 (Paperback)

Color reproduction by Media Development and Printing Ltd., UK
Printed and bound in China by L. Rex Printing Company Ltd.

Discover more at
www.dk.com
www.starwars.com

Contents

DK READERS

READING 3 ALONE

STAR WARS

BATTLE FOR NABOO

Written by Lisa Stock

Trouble brewing

For many years, the great Republic has united thousands of planets in the galaxy. These planets are ruled peacefully by an elected body called the Senate. Arguments between the planets are settled through discussions, not war.

The Senate

Representatives from all over the galaxy discuss important matters in the huge Senate building. They are known as senators.

However, a sinister figure in the galaxy has different ideas about how it should be ruled. This means trouble!

Planet of Naboo

A little planet called Naboo is about to find itself at the center of the galaxy's turmoil.

Naboo is home to two species—humans (the Naboo) and Gungans. The Naboo live above ground while the Gungans live mostly below the surface. Up until now the two groups have lived separately, and their lives have been safe and peaceful under the Republic's rule. Little do they know that is all about to change!

Senator Palpatine

Naboo's senator is named Palpatine. He is a respected politician, but is he really looking out for Naboo's best interests?

Battleship blockade

The Republic regulates trade in the galaxy. A greedy group of merchants, however, called the Trade Federation are not satisfied with the Republic's rules—they want more power. The Trade Federation's leaders create a blockade around Naboo, to force the Republic to change its rules.

The Trade Federation's ship controls a huge army of robot soldiers called battle droids.

Now Naboo is cut off from the galaxy. It may look like a simple trade dispute, but behind the scenes there is a much darker force at work.

Viceroy Nute Gunray
The Trade Federation's leader is a Neimoidian named Nute Gunray. He is greedy and willing to wage war to make his organization richer.

Revenge of the Sith

A secret mastermind is behind the Trade Federation's plot—Darth Sidious! Sidious is an evil Sith Lord who wants to take over the galaxy.

*Darth Sidious appears to the Trade
Federation leaders in a hologram.*

The Sith are guided by the dark side
of the Force. Sidious is the most
powerful Sith ever. He despises the
Republic and wants its power
for himself. He doesn't care
who or what gets in his way.
That's bad news for Naboo!

The Force
The Force is an invisible energy that is only
felt by certain beings with special powers.
Sith feed on the dark side of the Force.
Their sworn enemy, the Jedi, use the light side.

Sidious is hiding another secret. He has a dual identity. He is a Sith Lord—and he is also Senator Palpatine from Naboo. No one suspects Senator Palpatine's other identity. In fact, he's quite a popular politician. Greedy Sidious is more than willing to sacrifice his home planet for the sake of his galactic ambitions.

Sidious has trained a terrifying apprentice called Darth Maul.

Maul has gleaming yellow eyes like other Sith.

With scary tattoos on his face and horns on his head, Maul is a frightening figure. He is also a highly trained, deadly fighter.

Darth Sidious has found a very obedient apprentice in Darth Maul.

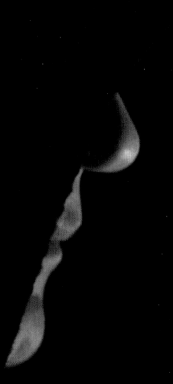

Obi-Wan Kenobi and Qui-Gon Jinn prepare for action.

Jedi to the rescue

The Jedi use the light side of the Force to protect the Republic. Their job is to keep the peace but they are also excellent fighters. The Jedi thought that they had destroyed the Sith centuries ago. But their old enemies are back— and they want revenge!

When news of the Naboo blockade reaches the Senate, Jedi Master Qui-Gon Jinn and his apprentice, Obi-Wan Kenobi, are sent to negotiate with Nute Gunray. But the Viceroy won't talk. Instead, Sidious orders him to destroy the Jedi and invade Naboo! Luckily, the Jedi escape into Naboo's swamps.

Jedi Master and apprentice face the might of the Trade Federation.

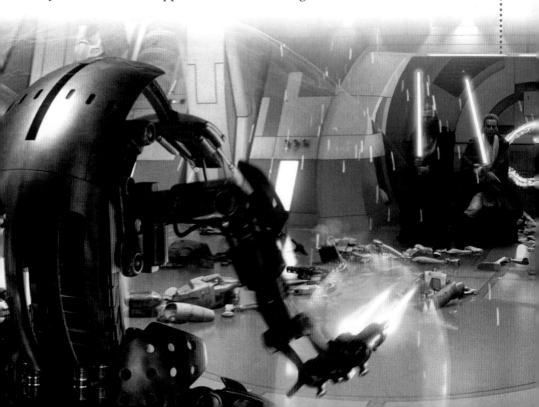

Young Queen

This is Naboo's ruler, Queen Amidala. She is very young but the Naboo trust her to rule them well from the planet's capital city, Theed.

When Amidala's beloved Naboo is attacked, she is taken prisoner. The Queen must save her people and her planet before it's too late. The Naboo don't have an army of their own. They need help fast. Maybe Naboo's other occupants, the Gungans, will come to the rescue?

Decoy Queen
When Queen Amidala is in danger she must hide her identity by using her handmaiden Sabé as a decoy.

Underwater world

Deep below Naboo's surface are the bubble-like domes of the Gungans' underwater cities. The Gungans are ruled by a High Council that meets in the city of Otoh Gunga. The Council's leader is Boss Nass. Gungans usually avoid contact with anyone outside their own species, particularly the Naboo.

The Gungans used to have a strong army but now they prefer to

The Gungan High Council

live quietly and in peace. How can they be talked into going to war again? It would mean being on the same side as the Naboo humans whom they do not trust. This is not going to be easy.

Boss Nass
The Gungan leader is stern but wise. He commands great respect from the Gungan population.

Gungan guide

Jar Jar Binks is a Gungan who was banished for bad behavior and now lives alone in the swamps.

Mottled skin

When Jedi Qui-Gon saves his life, Jar Jar promises to help the Jedi. At first Qui-Gon thinks he would be better off without this foolish Gungan. Yet he finds that Jar Jar can lead him to the Gungan Council. There they ask Boss Nass to help save Naboo. The meeting does not go well—the Gungans refuse.

Stubby feet

Obi-Wan and Qui-Gon meet Jar Jar in the swamps of Naboo.

The Jedi feel disappointed but they have no time to waste. They race to Theed to rescue Queen Amidala and then flee Naboo in the Queen's Royal Starship. But their ship is badly damaged by the blaster cannon from a Trade Federation ship.

Nervous navigator
Jar Jar tends to panic, which makes him a less than useful guide. He is also terrified of the giant sea creatures that chase him!

Boy hero

Anakin Skywalker is a young slave boy from the planet Tatooine, owned by a nasty junk merchant. He wants to be free to live a life of adventure!

The Jedi, Jar Jar, and Queen Amidala land on Tatooine in search of a new part for their damaged ship.

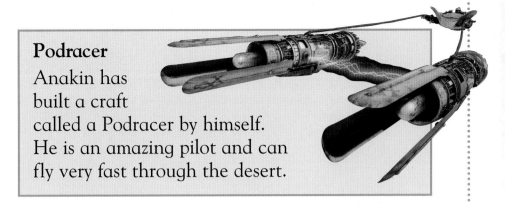

Podracer
Anakin has built a craft called a Podracer by himself. He is an amazing pilot and can fly very fast through the desert.

They soon come across Anakin and realize that he is a very special boy. Anakin puts his Podracing skills into action, winning a race so that the Jedi can buy the part they need. Anakin also wins his freedom. His life will never be the same again.

The Royal Starship is stranded briefly in the Tatooine desert.

Jedi and Sith fight a vicious duel.

Fight on Tatooine

Oh no! The Jedi won't be leaving Tatooine just yet! First they encounter an old enemy. Darth Maul is under orders to destroy the Jedi and capture Queen Amidala.

The Sith warrior attacks Qui-Gon, but the Jedi jumps to safety on the starship.

Finally, the Queen makes it to the Senate to ask for help. Despite her pleas on Naboo's behalf, the Republic's leaders don't want to rush into action.

Palpatine is one step ahead. He seizes the opportunity to manipulate Amidala. He persuades her to ask for new leadership in the Senate and then puts himself forward for the job. It's all part of the Sith Lord's evil plan!

Palpatine persuades the Queen to do exactly what he wants.

New alliance

If the Republic won't come to her aid, Queen Amidala must try again to persuade the Gungans to help save Naboo. Although the two species have lived separately for so long, joining forces is her only hope now.

At first Boss Nass is not happy to see visitors at the sacred place.

Jar Jar leads the Queen and the Jedi to the Gungans' sacred place. Amidala has been in disguise, but she reveals her true identity to Boss Nass to earn his trust. When he sees that she is sincere, he agrees to form an alliance against the Trade Federation. The Naboo and the Gungans will fight for their planet together!

Battle strategy

No one wants war—especially Queen Amidala. But sometimes fighting is the only option, even though there are great risks involved. Success on the battlefield depends on good preparation and clever tactics. Amidala has planned this battle very carefully. It is going to be fought in a few key locations across Naboo.

Queen Amidala's blaster

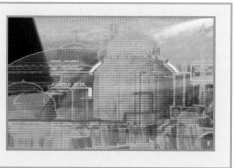

Holographic map
Queen Amidala is able to pinpoint the key locations of the battle on this three-dimensional map.

Using a holographic map, Amidala tells the Jedi, the Gungans, and the Naboo guards exactly what to do. With their help, hopefully she can defeat the Trade Federation.

Holographic map

The Droid Army

The Trade Federation uses a Droid Army to fight its battles. Droids make good soldiers because they always obey orders and never get tired. If they are destroyed, they can be easily replaced. Droids are easy to defeat in a one-on-one fight because they are not very smart.

Blaster

Flimsy body

But when many droids attack at once they are deadly. The Trade Federation sends most of its Droid Army to fight against the Gungans. They don't know this battle is only a diversion for a sneak attack on Theed Palace!

Droid Control Ship
The best way to stop the droids is by destroying the Droid Control Ship.

Gungans vs. droids

The Gungans are not used to fighting on land, but they bravely face the Droid Army on Naboo's grassy plains. The Gungan Army uses a protective shield so at first the tanks' blaster bolts cannot get through. When the Trade Federation realizes that its attack is not harming the Gungans, it changes its strategy.

The Gungans think they are protected by an energy shield that deflects enemy weapons.

Instead, the battle droids march forward and simply walk through the Gungans' shield. Uh-oh! In hand-to-hand combat this many droids will be hard to beat. To win, each Gungan will have to defeat dozens of droids!

The Gungans are certainly fulfilling their part of Amidala's plan by distracting the Trade Federation. Gungan warriors use giant catapults to throw plasma balls at the droids. The droids return fire with powerful blaster rifles.

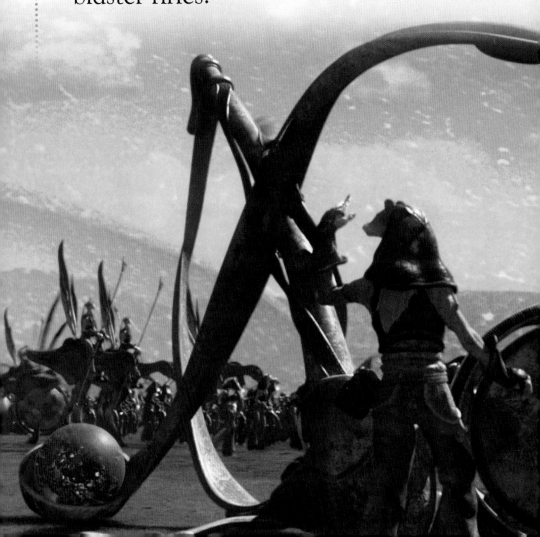

Battle droids use flying machines called STAPs.

The Gungans are outnumbered!
Can they keep up the fight long
enough for Queen Amidala to carry
out her clever plan?

Hero Jar Jar
Jar Jar's clumsiness
can be handy. He
accidentally sends a
load of energy balls
smashing into a
pack of battle droids
and tanks. Boom!

Hangar battle

While the battle on the grassy
plains rages, Queen Amidala,
the Jedi, and Anakin are busy at
Theed Palace. First they sneak into
the Palace's starfighter hangar.

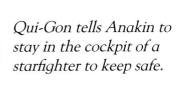

Qui-Gon tells Anakin to stay in the cockpit of a starfighter to keep safe.

The Jedi then fight off the droids—this allows Naboo pilots to take off into space to destroy the Droid Control Ship. Anakin accidentally starts a starfighter's engine and he takes off, too, firing at droid fighters. That's not what Qui-Gon had in mind!

Pilot Anakin
Thanks to his Podracing experiences on Tatooine, Anakin isn't scared to fly solo above Naboo.

Into the Palace

The next stage in Queen Amidala's plan is to take the Neimoidian Viceroy prisoner. She scales the walls with her guards and almost makes it to the throne room. But—disaster—they are all taken prisoner by droids!

The Queen sends an urgent
distress signal to Sabé, who rushes
to her aid. Sabé's arrival confuses
Nute Gunray, because she is dressed
as the Queen. The mix-up gives
the real Queen Amidala the chance
to rearm and capture Gunray!
The Viceroy has no choice but
to surrender!

Sabé arrives just in time to rescue the Queen.

Space battle

Naboo starfighter pilots are trying to destroy the Droid Control Ship. They are under attack from the Trade Federation's vulture droids. But here comes Anakin! The young pilot crash-lands inside the Droid Control Ship. Then he accidentally fires a pair of torpedoes into the main reactors! There is a huge explosion and the Trade Federation's ship is blown in half, just as Anakin escapes. All the battle droids are deactivated on Naboo. Anakin has saved the day!

Vulture droid
Vulture droids are droid aircraft. They shoot at starfighters, causing them to spin out of control and crash.

*Two Jedi against one Sith—
but the Jedi are still struggling.*

Sith duels

After his failure to stop the Jedi on
Tatooine, Darth Maul attacks them
again on Naboo. This time he's
determined to finish them off.

A lightsaber battle is deadly.
Qui-Gon and Obi-Wan take on
Darth Maul in a furious fight within
Theed's Generator Core—a very
dangerous place!

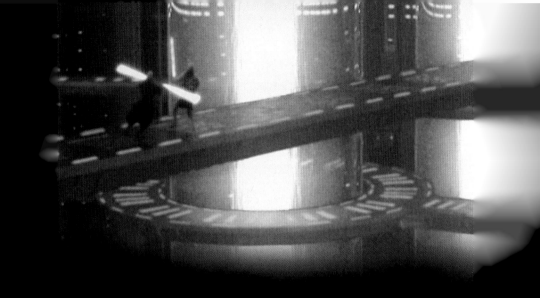

Both Jedi and Sith must focus their Force powers to help them win the battle. Feeding on the Force enables them to increase their strength and to sense what their opponent is going to do next. Unfortunately for the Jedi, Maul's lightsaber has two blades. That makes him twice as fierce!

Lightsabers

Lightsabers are special weapons used by Jedi and Sith. They are also known as laser swords.

An energy shield stops Obi-Wan in his tracks.

Qui-Gon is fighting the fiendishly strong Darth Maul alone. Obi-Wan is trapped behind an energy shield. He watches heartbroken as Maul fatally wounds Qui-Gon Jinn.

Obi-Wan must now fight Darth Maul to the death. The Sith apprentice is not so lucky this time...

After losing his
own weapon,
Obi-Wan uses
his Force powers
to summon his
Master's lightsaber.

*Obi-Wan tries to avenge
his Master's death.*

Spurred on by grief for his friend,
Obi-Wan swiftly wounds his evil
opponent. Maul is defeated.

As Qui-Gon takes his final breath,
he makes Obi-Wan promise to train
Anakin in the ways of the Jedi.
Qui-Gon believes that Anakin will be
a great Jedi one day.
Maybe he will be
the one to finally
bring balance to
the two sides of
the Force?

Celebration time

The battle for Naboo is over!
The planet is ruled by its loyal Queen
Amidala once more. The Naboo and
Gungans join together again for a
celebration parade on the streets of
Theed. Peace is restored—but at
what cost to the galaxy?

Trainee Jedi
Anakin is now officially a
Padawan, a Jedi in training.
He has lots of hard work ahead.

Palpatine has used the conflict to secure a new role for himself as Chancellor. He is one step closer to destroying the Republic. This peace is not going to last very long...

The Queen gives Boss Nass a gift of thanks from the Naboo.

Palatine has used the conflict to secure a new role for himself as Chancellor. He is one step closer to destroying the Republic. This peace is not going to last very long...

The Queen gives Boss Nass a gift of thanks from the Naboo.

DK READERS

READING 3 ALONE

Can the Jedi help to save
Naboo and prevent war in
the galaxy?

DK READERS

Stunning photographs combine with lively illustrations and
engaging, age-appropriate stories in DK READERS, a multilevel
reading program guaranteed to capture children's interest
while developing their reading skills and general knowledge.

LEARNING pre-level TO READ	Learning to read	○ High-frequency words ○ Picture word strips, picture glossary, and simple index ○ Labels to introduce and reinforce vocabulary ○ High level of adult participation helpful
BEGINNING 1 TO READ	Beginning to read	● Simple sentences and limited vocabulary ● Picture glossary and simple index ● Adult participation helpful
BEGINNING 2 TO READ ALONE	Beginning to read alone	● Longer sentences and increased vocabulary ● Information boxes full of extra fun facts ● Simple index ● C
READING 3 ALONE	Reading alone	● M ● Information boxes and alphabetical glossary ● Comprehensive index
PROFICIENT 4 READERS	Proficient readers	● Rich vocabulary and challenging sentence structure ● Additional information and alphabetical glossary ● Comprehensive index

With DK READERS, children
will learn to read—then read to learn!

Printed in China

$3.99 USA
$4.99 Canada

Visit the official website:
starwars.com

© 2012 Lucasfilm Ltd. and TM.
All Rights Reserved.
Used Under Authorization.

Discover more at
www.dk.com

ISBN 978-0-7566-9008-3

9 780756 690083